The Adventurous Chef: Alexis Soyer

Ann Arnold

FRANCES FOSTER BOOKS
FARRAR STRAUS GIROUX
NEW YORK

for
Sheila

Library of Congress Cataloging-in-Publication Data
Arnold, Ann.
    The adventurous chef : Alexis Soyer / Ann Arnold.
        p. cm.
    Summary: A biography of a flamboyant, successful French chef and
inventor of kitchen tools who opened soup kitchens during the Irish
potato famine and taught the army how to feed itself during the Crimean
War.
    ISBN 0-374-31665-1
    1. Soyer, Alexis, 1809–1858—Juvenile literature. 2. Cooks—
Biography—Juvenile literature. [1. Soyer, Alexis, 1809–1858. 2. Cooks.]
I. Title.

TX649.S6 A75 2002
641.5'092—dc21

                                                2002019224

KINGDOM of SWEDEN and NORWAY

NORTH SEA

BALTIC SEA

RUSSIAN EMPIRE

SCOTLAND

IRELAND
DUBLIN

WALES

ENGLAND
LONDON

ATLANTIC OCEAN

ENGLISH CHANNEL

KINGDOM of DENMARK

KINGDOM of HOLLAND

KINGDOM of BELGIUM
BRUSSELS

KINGDOM of PRUSSIA

PARIS MEAUX

FRENCH REPUBLIC

MINOR GERMAN STATES

AUSTRIAN EMPIRE

SWITZERLAND

PIEDMONT

PARMA

MODENA

MOLDAVIA

WALLACHIA

SERBIA

CONSTANTINOPLE

CRIMEA
Balaclava

SEA OF AZOV

BLACK SEA

Marseilles

KINGDOM of PORTUGAL

KINGDOM of SPAIN

SARDINIA

CORSICA

TUSCANY

ROMAN REPUBLIC

ADRIATIC SEA

KINGDOM of NAPLES

SICILY

OTTOMAN EMPIRE

BOSPORUS SCUTARI

AEGEAN SEA

IONIAN ISLANDS (BRITISH)

KINGDOM of GREECE
ATHENS

TURKEY

CRETE

MEDITERRANEAN SEA

NORTH AFRICA

N
W   E
S

Soyer's Travels

1821 Meaux to Paris
1831 Paris to London
1842 London to Brussels
1847 London to Dublin
1855 London to Scutari via Paris, Marseilles,
       Corsica, Athens, and Constantinople
1855 Scutari to Balaclava
1857 Balaclava to London via Meaux and Paris

O**N OCTOBER FOURTEENTH OF 1809,**
in the small French town of Meaux, famous for its cheese,

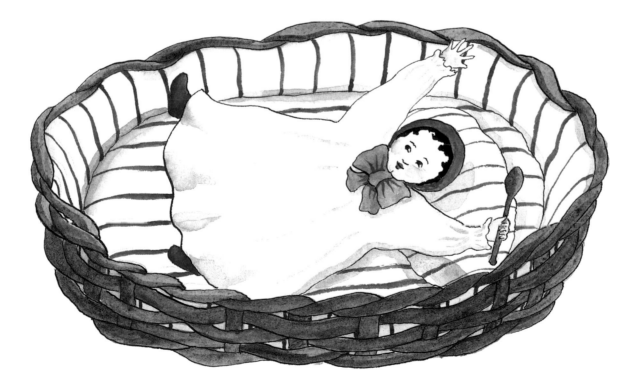

Alexis Benoît Soyer was born.
His mother and father kept a shop. Alexis was their third son.

He was bright and curious. When he turned nine, he was sent to the cathedral school. His mother hoped he would become a priest.

At school, Alexis loved the music but *not* the rules. He thought of a plan to escape. One midnight he rang the great church bell—it was also the local fire alarm.

The entire garrison turned out.
People ran from their houses in fear.

The whole town was in an UPROAR!
Alexis was expelled from school, of course. It was his first thoroughly
successful practical joke. He was twelve years old and in disgrace at home.

His brother Philippe, who was a chef in Paris, wrote to him: "Come be my apprentice. With your gifts, if you work hard, you could reach the top of our profession."

By the time he was seventeen, Alexis was directing a staff of twelve cooks. He kept them in good spirits with his amusing ways.

One day he told Philippe, "Now that I am a chef, I will dress as I please!"

He called his style "à la Zoug-Zoug," the cloth being cut on the bias so that the stripes ran diagonally. He wore his hat at a raffish angle, loose and floppy.

Alexis Soyer.
Chef de Cuisine.   Paris.

Even the shape of his calling card was unconventional.

In 1831 Philippe went to England to seek his fortune. He had taste, training, experience, and a French accent—in short, all that was necessary to become head cook in an aristocratic English household. Soon he was chef to the Duke of Cambridge.

He wrote to Alexis, "Come join me in the land where the French chef is king. You may choose your lord and name your price."

Alexis sailed at once. At first he worked with his brother creating elaborate menus for the Duke of Cambridge's frequent dinner parties.

Then the Duke of Sutherland asked him to join his staff. Soyer went on to work for several other noblemen and gentlemen.

The Marquis of Waterford

Mr. Lloyd of Aston Hall

The Marquis of Ailsa

His reputation spread. In 1837 he was offered the position of chef de cuisine at the newly created Reform Club in London. Soyer accepted on the condition that he and the architect would design the kitchen together. When they met, Soyer explained his conception. "Let us create a kitchen of spotless efficiency. No detail shall be left to chance. The fish shall be kept on an iced marble slab to retain its freshness. Fruits and vegetables shall be stored in labeled bins. Dinner plates shall be kept warmed and ready for serving in chambers beside the gas stoves—"

"Gas stoves?!" the architect exclaimed.

"But of course," Soyer replied. "I insist upon this new gas. It produces a flame that is easier to control and cleaner than wood or coal—with far less labor."

"These are excellent ideas," the architect agreed. "Your enthusiasm and invention shall be allowed full scope."

In time the Reform Club kitchens became one of the famous sights of London.

THE KITCHENS OF THE REFORM CLUB

A   Chef's office

B   Butchery ~ where meat is trimmed for cooking

C   Meat and game larder

D   Cold meat and sauce larder ~ with self-closing doors to keep out flies

E   Pastry and confectionery ~ with cool marble tables and steam-heated drawers

F   Cool hallway ~ with sloping marble table chilled by ice water to keep fish and seafood fresh

G   Roasting kitchen ~ with fireplace for roasting large pieces of meat and heating water

H   Vegetable kitchen and dishwashing sinks

I   Scouring scullery ~ where copper pots and pans are scrubbed and polished

J   Butler's pantry ~ where silver is counted and polished

K   Lift ~ for conveying food to the dining room above

L   Main kitchen

       1. Twelve-sided table to accommodate twelve cooks at once

       2. Small fire chamber for roasting

       3. Warm holding place for completed dishes

       4. Clerk's station ~ orders from the dining room are received through
          a speaking tube and relayed to the cooks

       5. Small grills for steaks and chops

The meals that emerged from the Reform Club kitchen were memorable, but Soyer was not just content to cook. His restless mind was always seeking improvements, and his desk at the Reform Club was cluttered with drawings and models of his various inventions.

The Drowning Ice-skater's Friend

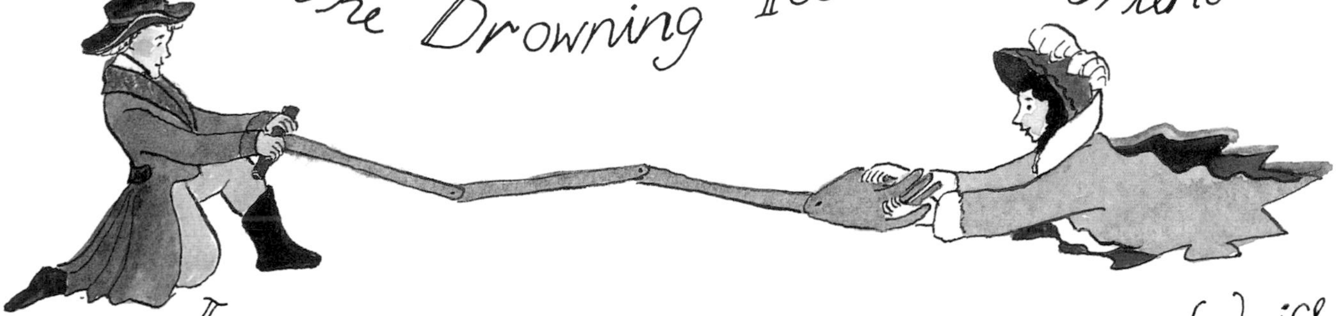

Inspired by Soyer falling through cracked ice into the River Thames

Presto-Change-O Suit

Sailor's Pivot Trivet

A two-way pivoting pot support for use in ships' galleys

A suit that changed from daytime to evening wear with the pull of a string

Multi-egg Poacher

Soyer's Magic Coffeepot

Soyer's Nectar

Drainer A
is placed inside pan B, which is
half-filled with boiling water.
Vegetables are added and boiled
rapidly until cooked. The cooked
vegetables are lifted out in drainer
and tamped with C to remove
excess liquid.

Pagodatique Entrée Dish with heated silver sand to keep food warm

Alarum Cooking Clock

Soyer's Timer

The first spring-operated kitchen timer

Lilliputian Magic Stove in use atop a Pyramid

Now that he was established as chef of the Reform Club, Soyer felt that he could afford to marry. He decided to send his portrait to a woman he knew in Paris, along with a proposal of marriage. But first he had to find a portrait painter. His secretary, Monsieur Volant, knew an artist and took Soyer to his house.

Monsieur Simonau welcomed his old friend Volant. When he learned the purpose of the visit, however, the artist suggested that Soyer would be better served by his stepdaughter. Miss Emma Jones, he claimed, excelled him in the art of portraiture. Matters were quickly arranged with Miss Jones, who was free to begin the very next day.

"Au revoir, Mademoiselle," Alexis said, kissing Miss Jones's hand, as was his custom. "Until tomorrow."

"Au revoir, until tomorrow," Emma answered, smiling quietly at Monsieur Soyer.

On the way home, Soyer confided to Volant, "I'm afraid having my portrait painted has become a pretext."

Volant stopped and looked at Alexis. "What do you mean?"

"Now that I am in love with Miss Emma, there is no need to send my portrait to Paris!" Soyer answered.

They both laughed and danced through the park arm in arm.

Emma Jones and Alexis Soyer were married in London on April 12, 1837. Emma painted, Alexis cooked, and they delighted in each other's company.

More and more people heard about the clever chef-inventor. One day the German Duke of Saxe-Coburg visited the Reform Club. Soyer showed him around the kitchen and put his inventions through their paces. Then Soyer led the Duke into his private room, where Emma's paintings now covered the walls.

The Duke was enchanted with all that he saw and invited Soyer to return with him to Brussels. He should bring some of Emma's paintings and his own kitchen devices to show the Duke's brother, the King of the Belgians.

But Soyer did not want to leave Emma, who would be having their first baby in a few weeks.

That evening Alexis and Emma discussed the day's events. He mentioned the Duke's invitation.

"It is impossible, of course," Soyer declared. "I wish to be here with you!"

"But you would return in time, Alexis! You must go. It is a great honor and you have been working so hard. This holiday is just what you need!"

"I would enjoy showing your paintings to the King," Soyer conceded.

"And your wonderful inventions, Alexis. How they would admire them in Brussels! You simply must go!"

So it was decided. On August 27, 1842, Soyer left London with the Duke of Saxe-Coburg. He would come home in time for their baby's arrival.

But it was not to be.

Two days later a violent thunderstorm broke over London, terrifying Emma. The windows rattled at each thunderclap; lightning cracked the sky. In her fright, Emma gave birth prematurely, and both she and the baby died.

Monsieur Volant traveled to Brussels to break the terrible news and bring Alexis back to London.

Soyer could not forgive himself for having left his wife's side. "I will never marry again," he insisted as he sat with Volant in his private quarters at the Reform Club, surrounded by Emma's paintings. "I could never find a woman like Emma. She shone as a painter, as a musician, as a housewife, and had a hundred other amiable qualities. What a treasure she was! Only cooking keeps me from complete despair!"

And so he worked more intently than ever.

Each day Soyer prepared elaborate meals at the Reform Club for the influential and the rich. And every evening as he returned home, he saw the poor and hungry begging for food on the streets of London.

"I will cook for these people as well," Soyer decided.

He began teaching charitable ladies to make nutritious soup to feed the hungry poor. Florence Nightingale's aunt was one of his first pupils.

Leave the peel on the carrot!

But Soyer wanted to do more. With the aid of the vicar of a local parish church, he opened a small soup kitchen where he could feed two or three hundred people each day. He worked on designs for a soup-boiler and a kitchen that could serve thousands.

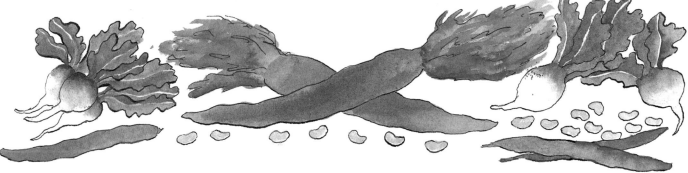

Yet still the ranks of the hungry grew. In 1845 a blight destroyed the potato crop in Ireland. Most people in Ireland lived almost entirely on potatoes and more than a million people died of starvation. The British government asked Soyer to build one of his soup kitchens in Dublin.

Nothing like it had been organized on such a scale before. "Nine thousand meals a day can be made in this kitchen alone," Soyer explained.

"And with the help of carts and barrows with fires beneath them, my hot soup can be taken all over town."

To help the poor feed themselves, he compiled *A Shilling Cookery for the People*.

He also published *The Gastronomic Regenerator*, a recipe book for the wealthy — or rather for their cooks.

And for the people in between he wrote *The Modern Housewife*. "I will help everyone to eat well," he would say.

The food is so badly cooked here that we cannot eat it. Many soldiers have died of starvation. We have no cooks, so we must cook for ourselves. But none of us knows how to do it. Please send us recipes so that we can use our rations well, Mr. Soyer.
Yours faithfully,
Edward Smith

While Soyer was feeding the rich and the poor in England, no one was properly nourishing the British soldiers far off in the Crimea, where France, Turkey, and Britain were at war with Russia. In 1855, after a year of combat, one miserable soldier wrote to Soyer: "The food is so badly cooked here that we cannot eat it . . ."

Soyer said to himself, "I will send recipes, yes—and, if I can do things *my* way, I will go there myself!"

Four months before, *The Times* had reported on the appalling conditions in the Crimean hospitals, where soldiers were dying from septic wounds, contaminated water, frostbite, and neglect. In response, the British government had sent Florence Nightingale and her nurses to the Turkish city of Scutari.

With starvation added to the soldiers' miseries, the government agreed to Soyer's proposal. Within the week Soyer sailed for Turkey with the first of his large portable camp stoves, four cooks, and the authority to act as he thought best. Stoves for all the troops were ordered to follow as quickly as possible.

When he arrived in Scutari, an aide-de-camp led him through the filthy streets to the hospital. There he was greeted by Florence Nightingale and her fellow nurses.

He found the hospital kitchens noisy, dirty, smoky, and chaotic; the smell of charred food lingered in the air. People were delighted by the arrival of the flamboyant chef; everyone was eager to learn from him.

Soyer called in bricklayers to rebuild the smoking chimneys. He had the giant copper cauldrons retinned so that food would no longer be tainted by verdigris. He told the purveyors, "This wet coal dust will never do as fuel. And these ancient chickens!" Soon the charcoal improved and the old fowls grew amazingly younger.

He posted his recipes on the kitchen walls. Now everyone was following the same plan.

Using ingredients at hand without added expense, he taught the soldiers to cook.

Before Soyer   After Soyer

Each orderly tied buttons, an old fork, or whatever to their men's joint of meat to identify it after cooking. Soyer replaced the oddments used to mark the meat with numbered skewers.

The meat was lashed tightly in bundles. The outer parts were boiled to shreds; the inner parts remained raw. Soyer had the joints of meat hung separately so that they could cook evenly and be ready at the same time.

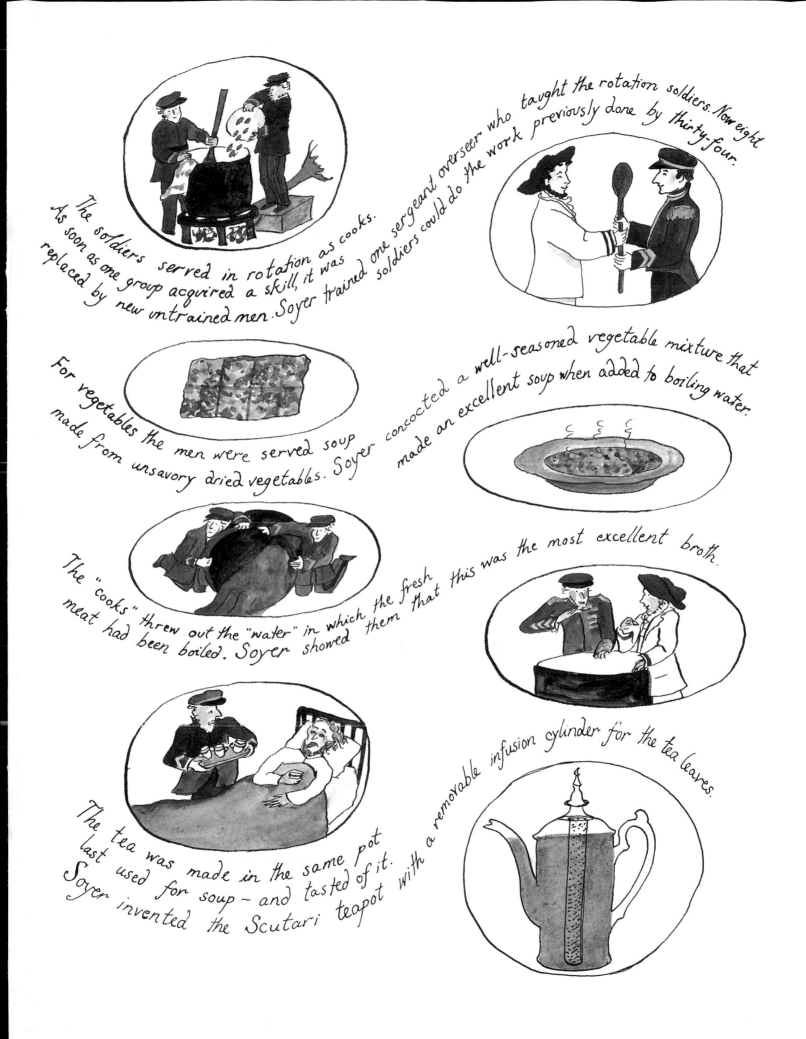

The soldiers served in rotation as cooks. As soon as one group acquired a skill, it was replaced by new untrained men. Soyer trained one sergeant overseer who taught the rotation soldiers. Now eight soldiers could do the work previously done by thirty-four.

For vegetables the men were served soup made from unsavory dried vegetables. Soyer concocted a well-seasoned vegetable mixture that made an excellent soup when added to boiling water.

The "cooks" threw out the "water" in which the fresh meat had been boiled. Soyer showed them that this was the most excellent broth.

The tea was made in the same pot last used for soup — and tasted of it. Soyer invented the Scutari teapot with a removable infusion cylinder for the tea leaves.

Miss Nightingale had brought nurses, cleanliness, and order to the hospital in Scutari. Under Soyer's leadership, the hospital kitchens began producing excellent meals for the sick and wounded. Now the two could sail together for the battlefields of the Crimea.

When they arrived, there was no suitable dwelling for them in Balaclava, so they slept aboard whatever ship happened to be at anchor.

Every day Soyer mounted his pony and visited the regiments. He handed out recipes and instructed the men in the most efficient and delicious way to use their rations. When equipment was lacking, he cajoled the suppliers into providing it. His cheerful, comical ways encouraged the troops.

Miss Nightingale, alas, soon caught Crimean fever and lay in bed, very ill. Soyer waited for news from the sanatorium where she was confined. When Miss Nightingale could eat again, he brought delicacies to her hospital bed every day.

The hard work, the mud, and the diseases of the battlefield left Soyer in a weakened condition. He, too, fell ill from Crimean fever and was sent to the hospital in Scutari. There the doctor warned him, "If you go back to the Crimea, take your tombstone with you! I strongly advise you to return to England immediately."

But Soyer replied that his work was not done. "I cannot leave until my stoves arrive and I have taught the soldiers to use them." He spent three months in bed, his case considered hopeless.

But the care of a young surgeon, Vincent Ambler, brought him to his feet. And now that he could cook for himself, his strength soon returned.

When Soyer learned that his stoves had arrived at the battlefront, he gathered his cooks together and sailed once again for Balaclava.

Before Soyer arrived, food was boiled in a large pot set on a tripod over an open fire. Most of the heat vanished into the air. Soon there were no trees left near the battlefields. Firewood had to be shipped to Balaclava, then carried in heavy carts drawn by horses through muddy roads to the temporary outdoor kitchens. The expense was enormous. Soyer's efficient stove, with its enclosed firebox, used a tenth the amount of fuel. A soldier could make a stack of pots inside the stove so that meat, potatoes, vegetables, and a pudding could all be steamed at the same time.

Soyer's stove was so successful that it was adopted by the entire army to be used at home and abroad, in times of war and peace.

After three years of bitter fighting, peace came to the Crimea in 1856. Everyone wanted to celebrate with feasts, and Soyer was as busy and sociable as ever.

He decided to give a farewell dinner for his fifty favorite friends. But everything seemed to go wrong. The plates and cutlery had gone astray; two of his cooks were ill; the singing club felt it could not perform without its two leading tenors, who had already left with their regiments. Even the turf that Soyer had laid out in front of his makeshift villarette had withered into brown wisps in the hot sun.

"Paint it green!" Soyer commanded his helpers. From then on, everything improved.

The utensils were found and the plates returned. Two volunteer cooks appeared. The singing club came in spite of its missing members and an army engineer provided a beautiful chandelier.

By candlelight, the painted grass looked perfectly natural. Of course, the food was superb.

As the few remaining guests mounted their horses at five the next morning, Soyer knew his last party had been the best of all.

It was time to go home.

Soyer packed his bags, his pots, and his pans and made his way to the
ship. In port he met a Russian orphan, who pleaded with Soyer to take him
to England. "I will be your servant," the boy vowed.

"You shall keep me company on the way home," Soyer replied.

By the time they reached England, Daniel Maximovitch Chimachenka
was a devoted attendant, dressed in a uniform of Soyer's design.

During the voyage, Soyer taught the boy English and the ways of the
kitchen. The chef also wrote a lively account of his Crimean adventures—he
called it *A Culinary Campaign*.

Florence Nightingale never fully recovered from Crimean fever. On her return to England, she took to her bed and rarely left it. From that bed, however, she reformed the British Army's barracks and hospitals throughout Britain and India. Her report for the Royal Commission on the Health of the British Army was blunt.

"Our soldiers enlist, to death in the barracks," she wrote. She appealed to Soyer. "The army will use your stoves, of course, but what are stoves without chefs? You must organize schools of regimental and hospital cookery, plan their kitchens, and devise recipes. There is so much to be done."

"I will begin at once, Mademoiselle." He wrote cookbooks, invented and tested an improved canning process for meat, and laid out a new model kitchen for the Wellington Barracks.

Although Crimean fever had also shattered Soyer's health, he refused to reduce his activities.

One day in the summer of 1857 he was invited to a picnic outside London. When the groom came with the horse, he warned Soyer, "Your stallion seems quite frisky this morning. Wouldn't you rather take the train?"

"I, who have traveled all over the Crimea on ponies and chargers and mules!"

Indignantly Soyer mounted and trotted off at a brisk clip . . . a little too fast, for the skittish horse was soon out of control. He tossed his rider to the ground, but Soyer's foot was caught in the stirrup, and he was dragged for many yards by one leg.

When his foot slipped free, Soyer was astonished to find he could stand up. He said to a member of the watching crowd, "Would you please call me a cab? I am late for a picnic. My friends will be worried!"

When Soyer appeared, he explained to the guests, "Forgive my disarray. I am a bit tattered and bruised but, you see, I was dragged quite a way by my horse. Nothing serious, however. It reminded me of the Crimea."

"Tell us, Soyer."

As Soyer left the picnic, he announced to his friends, "You will probably find me in bed for the next few days. Do come by for a visit."

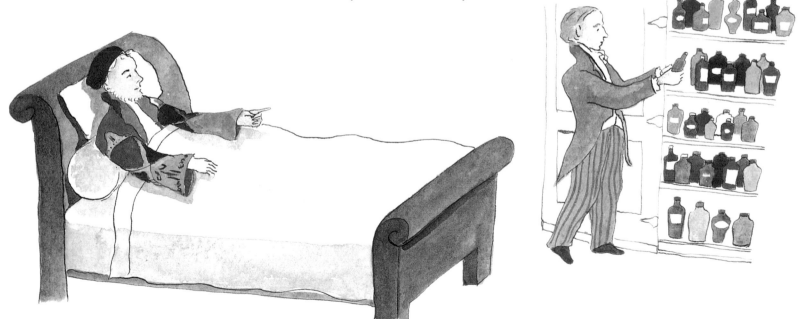

The doctors came as well. Soyer explained to Volant, "I do not put much faith in physicians, but I would not dream of hurting their feelings. I always hide Dr. A.'s medicine before Dr. B. arrives! Just put this bottle in the cupboard for me, please!"

In a few weeks Soyer felt better and was again as busy as ever. Dr. Ambler begged him to rest. But Soyer insisted upon opening his new kitchen at the Wellington Barracks. It would set an example for other military establishments.

On opening day a crowd of military officers gathered in the kitchen to watch Soyer turn basic army rations into a delicious dinner for three hundred men.

Soyer, ever playful, waved his hand toward his well-worn pots and pans. "Gentlemen, you have your battery of weapons; this is *my* Crimean *batterie de cuisine*. And now for our dinner!

"Instead of twice-boiled beef and watery broth, we will have green pea soup, salt pork and cabbage, roast mutton, beef dumplings, crisp potatoes, and rice pudding."

"This is splendid, Soyer!" exclaimed the admiring Lord Rokeby, a fellow veteran of the Crimea. "You must repeat this on a still larger scale. I would like to see you feed a whole battalion of the Guards."

But shortly after the feast for three hundred, Soyer fell ill again. The doctors came to see him as before, one after another.

Whenever Soyer felt just a little better, he would summon a few friends. "Do come! I will cook. Then we'll go to the theater. After that, on to Frost's for a bite to eat."

He would arrive home at dawn, tumble into bed, and remain there for days. He recovered eventually, but each time he was weaker. "Surely my cooking will make me well," he liked to think. "It has never failed me yet."

Again, he planned a dinner party, drew up the menu, invited the guests, and ordered dessert from town. But this last meal was never cooked. Alexis Soyer died in his bed on August 5, 1858.

Florence Nightingale

LONDON
3 PM
6 AU
1858

POSTAGE
ONE PENNY

Capt. Galton
War Office
London

August 1858

His death is a great disaster. Others have studied cooking for the purpose of gourmandising, some for show, but none but he for the purpose of cooking large quantities of food in the most nutritious manner for great numbers of men. He has no successor.